100 facts
Elephants

Camilla de la Bedoyere

Consultant: Steve Parker

Miles Kelly

First published as hardback in 2007 by Miles Kelly Publishing Ltd
Harding's Barn, Bardfield End Green, Thaxted, Essex, CM6 3PX

This edition printed 2012

4 6 8 10 9 7 5 3

Publishing Director: Belinda Gallagher
Creative Director: Jo Cowan
Volume Designer: Sally Lace
Image Manager: Lorraine King
Indexer: Jane Parker
Production Manager: Elizabeth Brunwin
Reprographics: Anthony Cambray, Liberty Newton, Ian Paulyn, Lorraine King
Assets: Lorraine King

ISBN 978-1-84810-102-9

Printed in China

British Library Cataloguing-in-Publication Data
A catalogue record for this book is available from the British Library

ACKNOWLEDGEMENTS
The publishers would like to thank the following artists who have contributed to this book:
Ian Jackson, Andrea Morandi, Eric Rowe, Mike Saunders, Mike White

All other artworks from the Miles Kelly Artwork Bank

The publishers would like to thank the following sources for the use of their photographs:
Cover Jurgen & Christine Sohns/FLPA; Page 14 Norma Cornes/Fotolia.com;
18(t) Karl Ammaman/naturepl.com, (b) Steve Meyfroidt/Fotolia.com;
22 Joël Dallio/Fotolia.com; 26 Konrad Wothe/Minden Pictures/FLPA;
28 TAOLMOR/Fotolia.com; 29 John Downer Productions/naturepl.com;
30(c) Bhupinder Singh/Fotolia.com; 32 Dr Dereck Bromhall/OSF;
35(b) Hulton Archive/Getty Images; 43 Joël Dallio/Fotolia.com; 44 Steve Turner/OSF;
46 Jason Maehl/Fotolia.com; 47(t) Mike Powles/OSF, (b) Reuters/Antony Njuguna

All other photographs are from:
Corbis, Corel, digitalSTOCK, digitalvision, Flat Earth, ILN, iStockphoto.com,
John Foxx, PhotoAlto, PhotoDisc, PhotoEssentials, PhotoPro, Stockbyte

Every effort has been made to acknowledge the source and copyright holder of each picture.
Miles Kelly Publishing apologises for any unintentional errors or omissions.

Made with paper from a sustainable forest

www.mileskelly.net
info@mileskelly.net

www.factsforprojects.com

100 facts
Elephants

Contents

Gentle giants

1 **Elephants are amazing creatures.** They are bigger than any other animals that live on land, yet their closest living relatives are no larger than rabbits. Elephants are powerful, but they are also sensitive, intelligent creatures that live in close, caring families. They are strong enough to topple a tree, but gentle enough to pick a flower with their trunks. These mighty beasts have been part of human history for centuries, but now they face an uncertain future.

▶ African savannah elephants walk slowly across the grassy plains. They live in close family groups called herds and spend most of their time eating and searching for food.

Elephant ancestors

2 **Elephants belong to an ancient family of animals that had long noses, or trunks.** Members of this family, called palaeomastodons, have become extinct (died out) except for three – African forest and savannah elephants and Asian elephants.

3 **One of the elephant's relatives looked like a pig with a long snout.** This odd-looking creature is called *Moeritherium*. It lived between 50 to 35 million years ago.

▼ These animals lived many millions of years ago in North Africa. They are the possible ancestors of modern elephants.

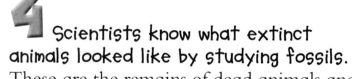

Moeritherium lived around 50 million years ago

4 **Scientists know what extinct animals looked like by studying fossils.** These are the remains of dead animals and other living things that turned into stone over millions of years. Usually, just hard parts such as bones and teeth survive as fossils.

5 **The remains of woolly mammoths have been found in blocks of ice.** These animals were relatives of modern elephants that became extinct about 10,000 years ago. Because the remains have never thawed out, they have been preserved in the ice.

◄ Woolly mammoths had thick, shaggy fur to keep them warm, small ears and enormous tusks.

Primelephas lived around
7 million years ago

6 **People hunted mammoths for food and fur.** Humans and mammoths lived in the Ice Age, when food was scarce. By working in groups to find, chase and kill mammoths and other animals, humans were able to survive this tough time.

▼ Columbian mammoths lived in North America, where the climate was less cold. Their bones, teeth and tusks have been found preserved in rock.

Palaeomastodon lived around
35 million years ago

I DON'T BELIEVE IT!

Mammoths preserved in rocks or ice probably died quickly. They may have fallen into lakes that froze, or got swept away in rivers before their bodies could be covered in mud and rot away.

7 **Not all mammoths were woolly.** The earliest ones lived more than four million years ago in grasslands. Here, the weather was warm so they didn't need thick fur. Mammoths were a very successful group of animals, and they lived in many parts of the world, probably in their millions.

Curious cousins

8 There is no living animal that looks like an elephant. To find out who their closest relatives are, scientists use clues, such as the type of teeth and bones that animals have. They have discovered that elephants have some strange relatives.

▲ Where there is plenty of food, manatees may live in groups of up to 100 animals.

9 Dugongs are huge, sea–dwelling animals. It is hard to believe that they are the closest living relatives of the elephant, but they share the same ancient ancestors. Dugongs eat plants underwater and come to the surface to breathe air.

10 Manatees, also known as sea cows, look similar to dugongs. They are also related to elephants. Manatees live along coasts and in fresh water, particularly in marshy areas, where they graze on plants. They can grow to over 4 metres long.

QUIZ

a. Dugongs and manatees live in the water. True or false?
b. Aardvarks are friendly animals that are easy to spot. True or false?
c. Hyraxes have beaks instead of teeth. True or false?

Answers:
a. True b. False c. False

► The DNA of this hyrax and that of elephants is quite similar. DNA is a substance found in animals' bodies. It has all the information needed to make an animal grow.

11 **Hyraxes may be the size of a rabbit, but they are the elephant's closest living relative.** The bones in their feet are similar to the elephant's, and they have tusklike teeth that keep growing all their lives. These little mammals eat plants and live in Africa and the Middle East.

12 **Aardvarks live in Africa, but they are so shy that little is known about them.** They live alone in burrows, only coming out at night to search for their favourite food of ants and termites. They probably had the same ancestor as elephants, many millions of years ago.

▼ Aardvarks bear little resemblence to elephants, but scientists believe the two are related.

► Elephant shrews use their long, flexible snouts to rummage through leaves, in search of food.

13 **Elephant shrews, tenrecs and golden moles may also be part of the elephant's wider family.** Elephant shrews are small African mammals that eat insects. Tenrecs live in Africa, and Madagascar. They have long snouts that are covered in sensitive hairs and eat insects, worms and grubs. Golden moles are rarely seen as they spend most of their lives in underground burrows.

Where in the world?

14 There are three main types of elephant – two African and one Asian. African elephants are larger and they can measure up to 5 metres in length. Both males and females have tusks, which are long teeth that grow out of the mouth on either side of the trunk. They only live in Africa, but they are found in many types of habitat.

▶ African savannah elephants have huge ears and long, curved tusks.

15 There are two types of African elephant – forest and savannah. Forest elephants have darker skin than those that live on the savannah. They also have yellow-brown tusks that point downwards rather than curve upwards, and their trunks can be quite hairy. Forest elephants live in areas where there is a lot of thick vegetation.

▲ Asian elephants usually have smaller tusks than their African cousins, and much smaller ears.

16 Asian elephants are found in India and other parts of Southeast Asia. Males can weigh over 5 tonnes and measure more than 3 metres from the toe to the shoulder. Female Asian elephants do not always have visible tusks and are smaller than the males. The teeth of Asian elephants are very like those of mammoths, and it is thought that these two animals are closely related.

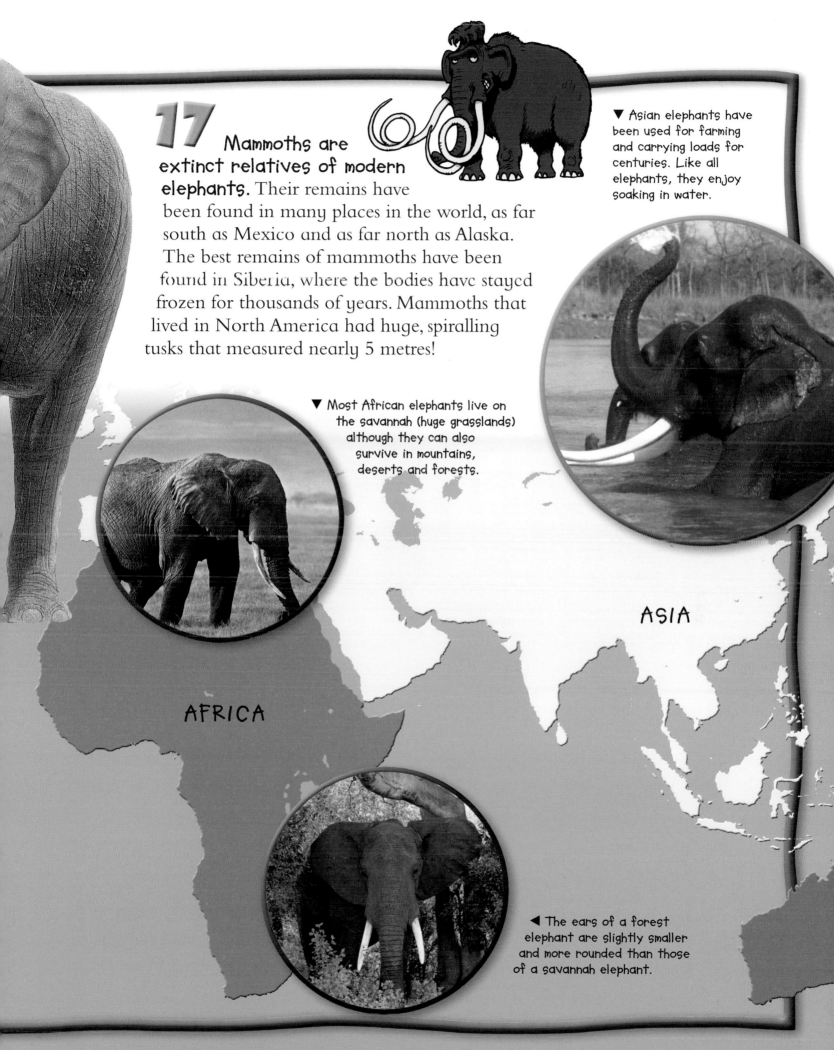

17 **Mammoths are extinct relatives of modern elephants.** Their remains have been found in many places in the world, as far south as Mexico and as far north as Alaska. The best remains of mammoths have been found in Siberia, where the bodies have stayed frozen for thousands of years. Mammoths that lived in North America had huge, spiralling tusks that measured nearly 5 metres!

▼ Asian elephants have been used for farming and carrying loads for centuries. Like all elephants, they enjoy soaking in water.

▼ Most African elephants live on the savannah (huge grasslands) although they can also survive in mountains, deserts and forests.

ASIA

AFRICA

◄ The ears of a forest elephant are slightly smaller and more rounded than those of a savannah elephant.

13

What a handy nose!

18 No animal on the planet has a nose quite like an elephant's! A trunk works like a nose, but it does so much more than just sniff at things. This is because it is more like an extra arm than a smelling organ. It is made up of the elephant's upper lip, nose and face muscles that have all joined together.

19 Elephants' trunks are packed with muscles, making them strong, bendy and very useful. They do not have any bones and that means they can move, stretch and curl in a way that limbs can't. A trunk is used for breathing and smelling, but it is also used for holding, grabbing, greeting and fighting.

◄ Elephant trunks developed over millions of years. Early ancestors used their smaller trunks like snorkels to breathe underwater.

African elephant

Asian elephant

▼ The inside of an elephant's trunk is packed with powerful muscles that surround two tubes – the nostrils.

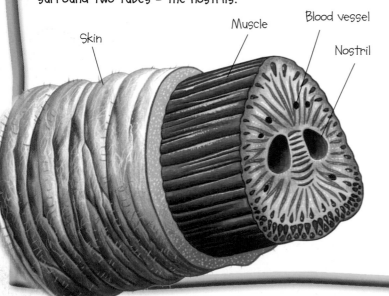

Skin

Muscle

Blood vessel

Nostril

▲ The trunk of an African elephant ends in two tips, whereas the trunk of the Asian has just one tip.

20 The trunks of African and Asian elephants are slightly different. An African elephant's trunk has two tips that work like fingers that can hold small things, such as a flower or a seed. The trunk of an Asian elephant only has one tip, but it can still pick up small objects.

21 **Without its trunk, an elephant would find it impossible to eat.** Trunks pull food from the ground or bushes, but they also reach into trees for leaves and fruit that other animals can't reach. Elephants have been known to use their trunks to throw stones at people, too!

▶ Trunks stretch and move in many directions. As well as for eating, an elephant uses its trunk to wipe an eye, spray water and blow air on its skin.

22 **An elephant pours water into its mouth with its trunk.** Trunks work like straws, letting elephants suck up water. Once its trunk is full, the elephant lifts its head up and back, holds its trunk high above its mouth, and lets the water pour out.

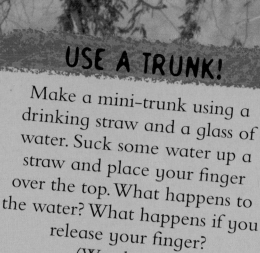

USE A TRUNK!

Make a mini-trunk using a drinking straw and a glass of water. Suck some water up a straw and place your finger over the top. What happens to the water? What happens if you release your finger?
(Watch out!)

23 **The trunk is so sensitive, an elephant can smell other animals that are far away.** A male uses his sense of smell to find a female mate. A female also uses her trunk to stroke her calf (baby) when she is feeding it, to calm it if it is anxious.

◀ If they are too hot, elephants use their trunks to spray their bodies with cooling mud or water.

Teeth and tusks

24 Elephants have unusual teeth that are ideal for chewing and grinding tough plants, such as bark and grass. They only have two front teeth – these are the tusks that grow long and curved. The other teeth are huge molars that are covered with ridges that help to mash food, breaking it into smaller pieces that can be swallowed.

25 Humans have two sets of teeth in their lifetime, but elephants have six. This is because their teeth wear out quickly due to all the chewing they have to do. Baby elephants are born with their first set of four molar teeth in their mouths. These have usually fallen out by the time the elephant is two years old, and a new set grows in their place.

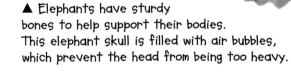

▲ Elephants have sturdy bones to help support their bodies. This elephant skull is filled with air bubbles, which prevent the head from being too heavy.

First molar

Second molar

Third molar

Fourth molar

Fifth molar

Sixth molar

▲ It is possible to work out how old an elephant is by looking at its teeth. By the time an elephant has its sixth molar, it is about 40 years old.

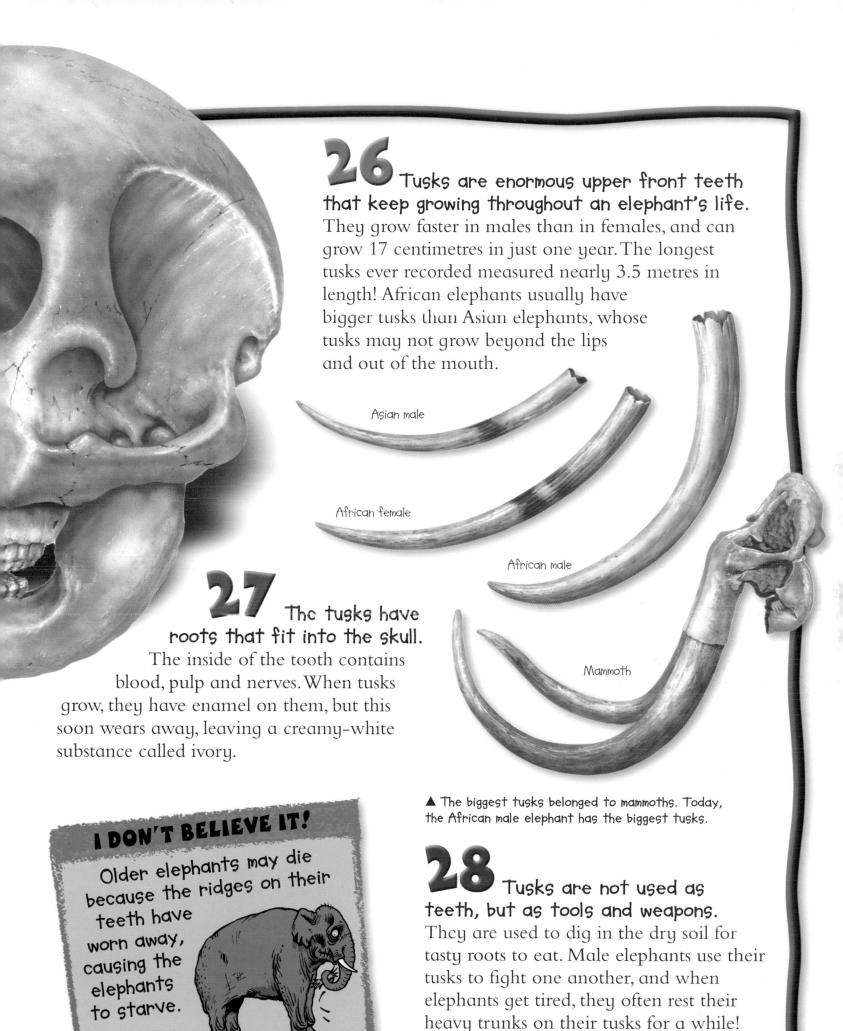

26 Tusks are enormous upper front teeth that keep growing throughout an elephant's life. They grow faster in males than in females, and can grow 17 centimetres in just one year. The longest tusks ever recorded measured nearly 3.5 metres in length! African elephants usually have bigger tusks than Asian elephants, whose tusks may not grow beyond the lips and out of the mouth.

Asian male

African female

African male

Mammoth

27 The tusks have roots that fit into the skull. The inside of the tooth contains blood, pulp and nerves. When tusks grow, they have enamel on them, but this soon wears away, leaving a creamy-white substance called ivory.

▲ The biggest tusks belonged to mammoths. Today, the African male elephant has the biggest tusks.

I DON'T BELIEVE IT!

Older elephants may die because the ridges on their teeth have worn away, causing the elephants to starve.

28 Tusks are not used as teeth, but as tools and weapons. They are used to dig in the dry soil for tasty roots to eat. Male elephants use their tusks to fight one another, and when elephants get tired, they often rest their heavy trunks on their tusks for a while!

Mighty meals

29 Elephants are herbivores, which means they only eat plants. However, plants are hard to digest (break down in the stomach and intestines). Getting goodness from plants is so difficult that herbivores spend most of their time eating and digesting food.

▼ Many trees that elephants like to eat are covered in spines. This elephant barely notices the prickly bits on this acacia bush.

30 Around two-thirds of an elephant's time is spent eating, and one elephant can get through 200 kilograms of food in a day. They eat grass, reeds, shrubs, leaves, branches, bark, flowers, fruits and seeds. Their trunks pull food from trees or the ground. They use their toenails and tusks to dig up tubers and roots.

QUIZ

Herbivores eat plants and carnivores eat meat. Do you know which of these animals are carnivores, and which are herbivores?

Tiger   Hippo   Owl
Dolphin

Answers:
Herbivore: hippo
Carnivores: tiger owl dolphin

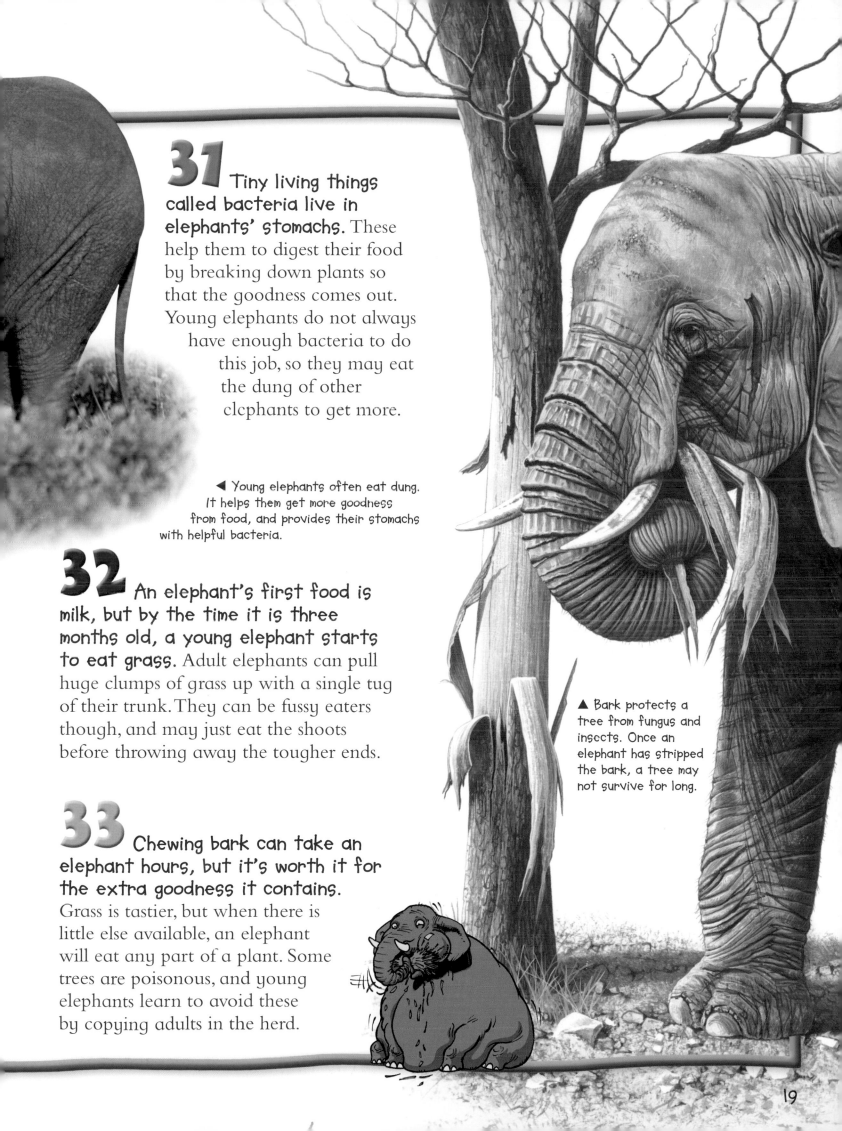

31 Tiny living things called bacteria live in elephants' stomachs. These help them to digest their food by breaking down plants so that the goodness comes out. Young elephants do not always have enough bacteria to do this job, so they may eat the dung of other elephants to get more.

◀ Young elephants often eat dung. It helps them get more goodness from food, and provides their stomachs with helpful bacteria.

32 An elephant's first food is milk, but by the time it is three months old, a young elephant starts to eat grass. Adult elephants can pull huge clumps of grass up with a single tug of their trunk. They can be fussy eaters though, and may just eat the shoots before throwing away the tougher ends.

▲ Bark protects a tree from fungus and insects. Once an elephant has stripped the bark, a tree may not survive for long.

33 Chewing bark can take an elephant hours, but it's worth it for the extra goodness it contains. Grass is tastier, but when there is little else available, an elephant will eat any part of a plant. Some trees are poisonous, and young elephants learn to avoid these by copying adults in the herd.

Fun at the waterhole

34 Elephants enjoy splashing in water, and a waterhole is a perfect place to cool down, drink, play and rest. Elephants live in hot places, and when they are feeling uncomfortable in the heat, they make their way to a waterhole or river to paddle, wallow and swim.

35 All elephants are excellent swimmers. They often dip below the water's surface using their trunks as snorkels to breathe. Some have even been seen to roll right over, so only the soles of their feet can be seen poking above the water!

36 Elephants are mammals. This means they have warm blood and give birth to live babies. Most mammals have fur to protect their skin from the sun and wind, but elephants have little body hair. This means that their skin can get dry and damaged. At a waterhole, elephants coat their skin in mud to cool and protect it.

▶ All elephants are usually grey in colour. They may appear to be brown or even reddish–brown if they have coated their skins in mud at a waterhole.

37 Elephants can use their ears like giant fans to cool down their whole bodies. The huge ears are full of blood vessels, and when an elephant flaps them, air moves all around, cooling the blood inside. The blood travels to other parts of the body, helping the elephant to control its temperature.

I DON'T BELIEVE IT!

Baby elephants can swim almost as soon as they can walk, and can even suckle (drink their mother's milk) while underwater.

Female elephants

38 Elephants live in family groups that are led by the females. A group of elephants is called a herd and the leader is called a matriarch. She is normally the oldest female and is related to all the other females and youngsters in the herd. The matriarch can use her great age and experience to protect the herd, and lead it to food and water.

39 Female elephants start their own families when they are aged about ten, and they have calves every four to six years. They stop having calves when they are about 60, but by then they are grandmothers, or even great-grandmothers, and they help to look after all the young elephants in a herd.

▲ These two young elephants obey the older females in their herd. If they are in trouble, or scared, they rely on the matriarch to protect them.

▲ Females work together to keep the herd safe. When threatened, older family members form a circle around the youngsters. When they walk in file, the youngsters stay close to the adults, who keep watch for predators.

40 Calves are looked after by all females in the herd. Females as young as six start to care for younger brothers or sisters. This is good practice for motherhood. When they are teenagers, females are shown how to attract males by their mothers and grandmothers.

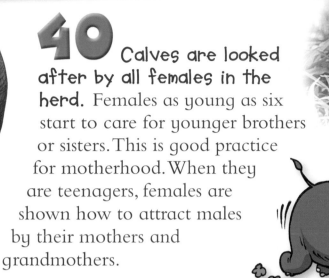

▲ This lion cub is at risk from female elephants, who know it may grow up to prey on elephant calves.

41 An African elephant called Nzou adopted a herd of buffaloes. She was an orphan elephant who grew up with buffaloes on a ranch. As she grew older, she became their leader and protected the females, but she started killing the males. The male buffaloes had to be moved and Nzou was left to rule her herd.

42 Female elephants can be aggressive. They may kill any lion cubs they come across on their travels. If an elephant sees lions near her calf, she will come running, trumpeting loudly to scare the lions away.

Bull elephants

43 Male elephants (bulls) leave their families when they are 10 to 15 years old. The females push them out of the herd, and never let them return. They spend their lives feeding, fighting and looking for females to mate with.

44 Young males join groups of other males, and start to learn how to be like them. Some live alone, but most try to tag along with a group of older males. They watch them as they fight for mates, and learn these important skills for themselves. They don't usually mate with females until they are about 25 years old.

► Adult male elephants are called bulls and they either live alone or in small groups of males. They are more unpredictable and aggressive than females.

I DON'T BELIEVE IT!

Elephants in musth may be aggressive. To prevent this, Asian elephants used to be given drugs, or less food. This stopped them going into musth.

▲ Baby elephants form close bonds with other youngsters in their herd. They often touch and smell one another.

50 Calves have short trunks, and they don't quite know what to do with them. Until they have practised using the muscles in their trunks, which can take several months, they are unable to control this extra limb. A calf can curl its trunk over its head when it feeds from its mother, but that's about all!

51 Newborns arc welcomed into the herd by all the family members. They are allowed to come close and sniff the baby and touch it gently, introducing themselves. Before long, the youngster will be able to play with its cousins, brothers and sisters.

52 Baby elephants continue to feed on their mother's milk until they are about four months old. During this time, the mother needs to eat and drink plenty of water and for this reason females usually give birth in the rainy season. The babies rely on their mothers for protection, food and affection for many years. If a mother elephant dies before her calf is two years old, it is unlikely the calf will survive.

QUIZ

Elephants are mammals. Which of these animals are also mammals and feed their babies on milk?

Mouse Dolphin Lizard
Emu Cat Worm

Answer:
The mouse, dolphin and cat are mammals and feed their babies on milk

Intelligent creatures

53 **Elephants have big brains and are intelligent animals.** Like humans, they are born fairly helpless and have a long 'childhood'. They need to learn how to communicate, how to live in a group, how to find food and water and how to stay safe from predators. This learning pays off, because some elephants live to the age of 70.

54 **These amazing animals are quick to learn new skills.** Elephants that live close to humans may learn to copy some of the things we do, such as turning on taps or opening doors. If elephants look in a mirror, they recognize the image as themselves. Most animals think they are looking at another animal.

▲ Adult females stand over youngsters while they nap. They know which direction the sun is shining, and move so that their shadows always cover the sleeping babies.

55 **Elephants can draw and doodle.** In the wild, they may pick up sticks and doodle in the sand but no one knows why they do this, or whether they enjoy doing it. Elephants in zoos have been given paintbrushes and paper and have made pictures, some of which sell for large amounts of money.

◀ Zoo elephants can pick up a paintbrush and paint. Many seem to enjoy doing this!

56 In the same way as humans and other intelligent animals, Elephants use tools. Mothers teach their youngsters how to strip branches from a tree and use them to swat irritating flies away. They also use sticks to scratch their backs, and pick up objects to play with, or throw.

57 Farmers may use electric fences to protect their crops from elephants. However, these clever creatures have been known to pick up logs, carry them to the fence and drop them on it. Once the fence has been smashed, the elephant can walk over it without getting a shock, and eat the food.

▼ Cameras disguised as heaps of dung have been used to film elephants. Scientists watch the films to find out more about how these intelligent animals behave.

Communication

58 **Elephants use different ways to communicate with one another, just like we do.** We can talk, but we also use body language. This is the expressions on our faces and the way we hold or move our bodies, which gives other people information about the way we are feeling. Elephants also use their voices and body language to communicate.

▶ When elephants show anger they use body language, such as flapping their ears and standing tall. These are signs to other animals, such as this baboon, that they should back away, quickly.

59 **When they are excited, angry or scared, elephants make loud trumpeting calls.** This is communication, and it works well when an elephant needs to let animals nearby know how it is feeling. Elephants make a trumpeting sound by blowing air through their trunks.

◀ A trumpeting elephant can be heard from up to 10 kilometres away.

I DON'T BELIEVE IT!

Zoo elephants need to keep their feet in good condition so they can 'listen' to vibrations. So keepers trim their nails and remove tough skin in an elephant pedicure!

▶ An elephant's feet are cushioned by soft layers that pick up sounds. When walking, the feet spread out under the animal's weight.

60 Elephants listen to each another with their feet. When elephants rumble, the noise can travel through the ground for up to 10 kilometres. Other elephants detect these sounds as vibrations, which pass into their feet, through their skeletons and up to their ears.

62 Trunks also help elephants to communicate with each other. They put their trunks in one another's mouths to say hello, and they show each other how they are feeling by the position of their trunks. Mothers even use their trunks to smack their calves!

61 We are not able to hear some of what elephants say to each other because the sounds they make are too low. When elephants huddle together in a group they may often be 'talking' to each other, or to elephants far away. They do this by rumbling in a deep voice.

▶ Elephants may greet one another by wrapping their trunks together. They sniff each other and rumble a greeting.

Salt-lovers

63 **A herd of elephants munches through tons of rock in some deep, dark caves.** The rock contains salt, which the elephants need for their bodies to work properly. Animals that only eat plants, such as elephants, can't always get enough salt and other minerals in their normal diet. One way to get salt is to eat or lick rocks that contain it.

64 **The caves shown here are inside a mountain called Mount Elgon, in Kenya, Africa.** The elephants that live nearby regularly visit the caves. They dig out rock with their tusks and trunks to get to the salt and minerals.

65 Elephants' tongues are not long enough to lick salt, so they break off pieces of rock to eat. They use their tusks to do this, and over the years they can wear them down to stumps. They eat the rock using their huge molar teeth, which grind it down into smaller chunks to swallow. Elephants have eaten so much rock, it's possible that the caves have been entirely created by elephants 'mining' them.

66 The elephants pass through pitch-black tunnels to reach the salty walls. They use their trunks to feel their way as they travel deep into the mountainside. They walk in single file, taking care to avoid deep holes and cracks in the rocky cave floor.

▲ All elephants need salt in their diet. When adult elephants set off to the salt caves, the young elephants follow them. They learn how to dig for salt by copying the adults.

I SPY SALT

Salt is an important part of human diets, but too much of it can damage our health. Look on the sides of cereal packets, or other foods, to see how much salt one serving contains. Do some foods have much more salt than others?

In our lives

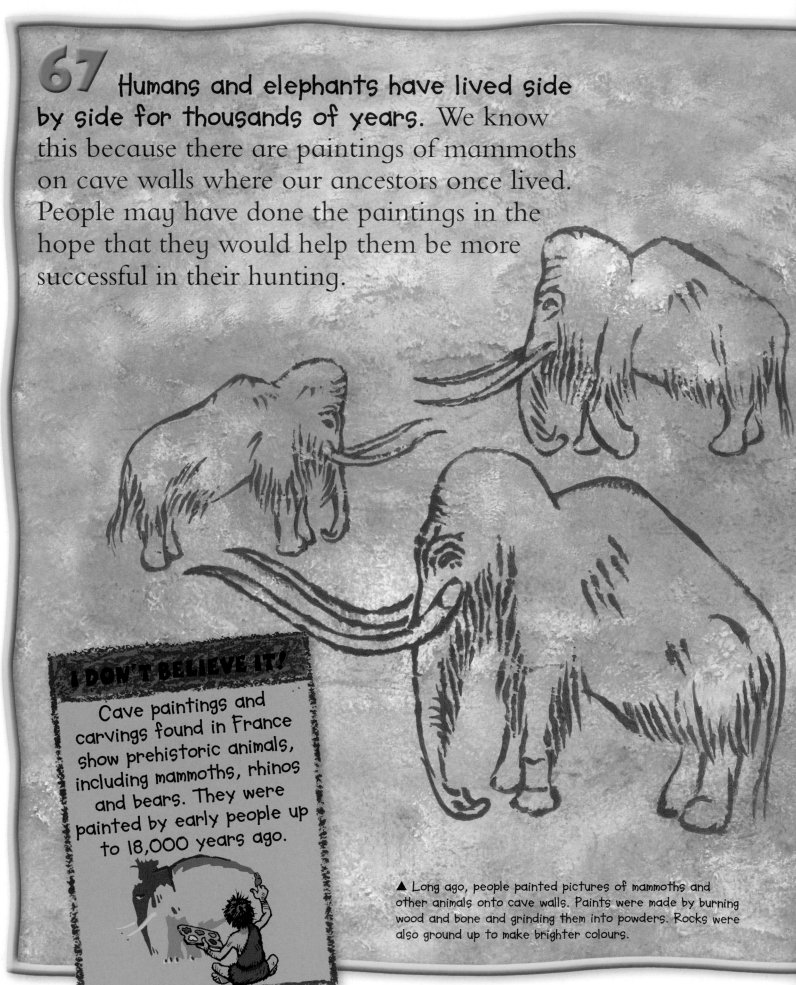

67 Humans and elephants have lived side by side for thousands of years. We know this because there are paintings of mammoths on cave walls where our ancestors once lived. People may have done the paintings in the hope that they would help them be more successful in their hunting.

I DON'T BELIEVE IT!

Cave paintings and carvings found in France show prehistoric animals, including mammoths, rhinos and bears. They were painted by early people up to 18,000 years ago.

▲ Long ago, people painted pictures of mammoths and other animals onto cave walls. Paints were made by burning wood and bone and grinding them into powders. Rocks were also ground up to make brighter colours.

68 Ganesha is the Hindu god of wisdom. He is shown in statues with a human body, four arms and an elephant's head. Every year in India, festivals are held to celebrate Ganesha's birth and colourful statues are dropped into the sea and rivers. People pray to Ganesha to ask for help on journeys and when they take exams.

▲ Ganesha has a pot-belly and just one tusk. He is often shown sitting or dancing.

▲ Elephant keepers take great care when painting their elephants for parades and festivals in India. They decorate the animal, hoping that it will be chosen as the best-dressed.

69 Decorating elephants is a popular form of artwork in many parts of Asia. Elephants are painted in bright colours and patterns, or decked in fine fabrics and jewels. During Elephant Day in Thailand, elephants are pampered at their own party, and treated to fruits such as watermelon, guava and papaya, which are given to them by well-wishers.

70 Jumbo was the most famous elephant that ever lived. He was captured in Africa in 1861 and was brought to Europe to be shown in zoos, where he was very popular. In 1881, Jumbo was sold to an American circus, but after just three years of travelling around the USA and Canada, Jumbo was killed on a railway by an express train.

▶ Jumbo's great size lead to the word 'jumbo' coming to mean 'big'.

The ivory trade

71 People have killed animals for millions of years. They are killed for meat to eat, and for fur and skins to provide warm clothing. More recently, animals are killed for less important reasons. Elephants have suffered because people value their white tusks, which are made of ivory.

▶ During the Ice Age, food was scarce. People laid traps and hunted in groups for mammoths. These huge beasts provided food, fur and ivory.

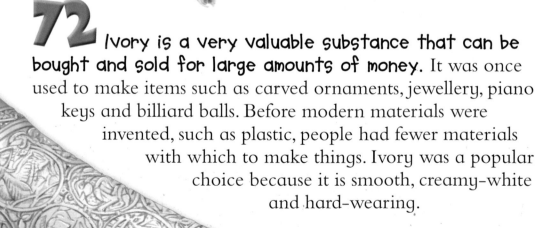

72 Ivory is a very valuable substance that can be bought and sold for large amounts of money. It was once used to make items such as carved ornaments, jewellery, piano keys and billiard balls. Before modern materials were invented, such as plastic, people had fewer materials with which to make things. Ivory was a popular choice because it is smooth, creamy-white and hard-wearing.

▲ A tusk can be carved with beautiful designs as it does not break or chip easily. Ivory ornaments are popular in Japan and other Asian countries.

▶ Mammoth tusks were used to make carvings of other animals, such as this early sculpture of a cormorant, a type of bird.

73 Ivory was first used to make tools and early pieces of sculpture.

There are ivory figures that were carved about 27,000 years ago by our ancestors. The tusks were probably taken from animals that had died naturally, or were killed for their meat. In recent times, elephants have been hunted and killed just for their tusks.

▶ Elephant hair bracelets are made with the tail hairs of elephants, which can reach one metre in length.

QUIZ

Ivory is a natural material. Which of these materials are natural, and which are man-made?

Wool Plastic Glass
Cotton Leather

Answer:
Wool, cotton and leather are natural, the others are man-made

74 Elephant hair is also used by people to make decorative objects. It is thick, coarse and long and can be turned into bracelets that are worn by Africans or sold to tourists. Hair is also used in some traditional medicines. The tough skin of an elephant can be treated, or cured, to become leather. Elephant leather is used to make shoes or fancy table tops.

Elephants at war

75 Before the days of planes and tanks, elephants were used in wars. Their height protected soldiers on their backs from attack, and few foot soldiers would have the courage to stand and fight in the face of an advancing army of elephants.

76 Hannibal was a general from Carthage, north Africa, who lived over 2000 years ago. He fought against the Romans and took an army of 50,000 men and 40 elephants over the Alps. He won three battles, but couldn't overthrow the Roman empire.

▲ Hannibal led his men and elephants over mountains. He headed into northern Italy and fought battles with the Romans, whose horses were scared of the enormous elephants.

I DON'T BELIEVE IT!

During the First World War, elephants were taken out of circuses and zoos and used to move heavy loads needed for building work.

77 The Romans used elephants to entertain people, as well as using them to fight their enemies. Elephants were put in arenas to fight one another, or were attacked by gladiators to amuse the huge crowds that gathered to watch. Elephants were also used in campaigns overseas, to help the Romans expand their empire. Many people had never even seen an elephant before the Romans attacked them!

▼ During campaigns, Roman soldiers strapped 'towers' to elephants' backs where they could shelter from their enemies' arrows.

◄ Even with its heavily armoured elephants to help, the Indian army failed to beat the British at the Battle of Plassey.

78 In 1757 the British army defeated a huge Indian army. About 2000 British soldiers were taken into battle by General Robert Clive, where they faced an Indian army of 50,000 men and several elephants. The British won the battle and increased their power in India, where they ruled for nearly 200 years.

At work and play

79 Thanks to their great intelligence and calm nature, elephants can be trained to help people work. They are used to lift and carry heavy objects, especially in places where vehicles and big machinery can't be used. Asian elephants have been logging for centuries – this involves moving huge logs that have been cut from trees in forests.

80 Elephants can be trained in different ways, some of which can be cruel. In the past, Asian elephant calves were taken from their mothers and chained to posts by their ankles. They were sometimes beaten until they learned to do what their trainers wanted.

81 Elephants can be trained to carry people on their backs and take them through forests, or across grasslands, looking for other animals. These animal safaris are very popular with tourists as they provide jobs for elephant trainers, and help to protect the environment from pollution.

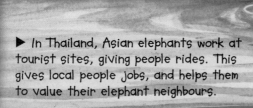
▶ In Thailand, Asian elephants work at tourist sites, giving people rides. This gives local people jobs, and helps them to value their elephant neighbours.

82 Elephants in Thailand were banned from logging work in the 1980s, because too much of the precious forests had been cut down. The elephants were left without any work to do, until they were taken to the cities to help with building work.

83 African elephants help vets get close to dangerous beasts, such as rhinos. When rhinos are ill and need medical help they can become dangerous. If a vet approaches on an elephant's back, the rhino remains calm and can be shot with a tranquilising dart. The dart sends the rhino to sleep while the vet takes care of it.

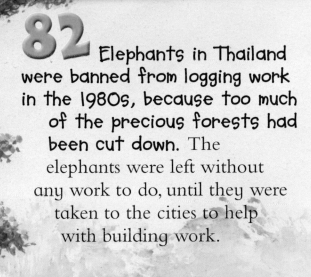

WORK THAT NOSE!

How easy would you find it to pick up a pencil using your nose and your upper lip? Would you be able to roll it along the floor with your nose? Try it and see!

84 Elephants don't just work, they get to play, too! In India and Nepal, elephants take part in a game called polo. Riders on their backs have long sticks that they use to hit balls across a pitch. The elephants are treated to drinks and nibbles at half time, and a dip in the river every day!

Keystone creatures

▼ Vultures are birds that feed on dead or rotting meat. When an elephant dies, its body is eaten by animals and birds, helping them to live and breed.

85 **Without elephants, other animals and plants would die.** For this reason they are called keystone creatures. Elephants help to shape the habitat (place they live), and this has an effect on other forms of life.

86 **As they stroll through forests or grasslands, elephants drop lots of dung.** The dung is full of coarse plant fibres that their bodies have not been able to digest. Seeds in the dung can begin to grow into new plants. In this way, elephants help to spread plants to new areas.

◄ This baboon finds a meal by picking out seeds and undigested plant matter from elephant dung.

87 **Some beetles gather elephant dung and roll it into a ball.** They lay their eggs in it and when the larvae (insect young) hatch, they eat it. Many other insects use dung as food, and without elephants they would be much rarer.

◄ Elephant dung, or manure, is like fertilizer for the soil. It contains many nutrients that animals, such as these dung beetles, and plants need to survive.

88 Elephants can damage farmers' crops as they search for food. Farmers often turn elephant feeding areas into fields, and the elephants do not understand that the new crops are not for them. If farmers plant rows of hot chilli bushes around their farms, the elephants stay away.

89 When a waterhole or river has dried up, elephants can dig to find water. They use their feet, trunks and tusks to remove soil until the water springs up. It is not only elephants who benefit from the water, but all the other animals nearby.

90 Elephants can destroy plants as they march through vegetation on the way to find food or water. For this reason many people think elephants do more harm to their habitat than good. But these pathways are useful for humans and other animals that need to get through dense forests. Elephants eventually change their routes, and the plants grow back.

▶ Elephants trample plants and bushes as they walk. The dead plants provide food for fungi, insects, worms and other forms of life that are, in turn, eaten by birds, lizards and mammals.

I DON'T BELIEVE IT!

Egrets are birds that like to hop about on the back of an elephant. They get a free ride, and can munch bugs and flies that dart around the elephant's feet.

Circle of life

91 All animals must die to make room on the planet for the next generation. Elephants live longer than most animals, but not all of them die of old age or disease. Like all wild creatures, they face dangers and difficulties – and survival can be a battle against the odds.

▼ No one knows how many elephants have been killed for their ivory. When ivory is found, it is taken by the government and destroyed so it can never be sold.

92 Humans have been taking the lives of elephants for hundreds of years. Now many populations of elephants are in danger of dying out completely. In the past, elephants were shot for sport and for their ivory. Nowadays they are more likely to lose their lives in the battle for space. In parts of Asia, especially, elephants are shot or electrocuted to keep them off farmland. They also get injured on roads and railways, or walk on unexploded landmines.

▲ Elephants sometimes visit the remains of a dead family member, touching the bones gently with their trunks.

93 It is possible to find the skeletons of several elephants near waterholes. This led to the belief in elephant graveyards, where elephants went to die. It's more likely that when some elephants are dying, they make their way to water, which they hope will make them better.

94 Elephants are known to grieve when a member of their family dies. When an elephant is dying, others try to help it get up. When it dies, members of the family stand around the body. They return to visit the body days later, and touch it gently with their trunks.

▶ Mothers have been known to stand by the bodies of their dead calves for up to three days.

Tomorrow's world

95 Elephants may not survive into the next century. The human population is growing in areas where elephants live, and their habitats are being turned into farms. In some places there is little food for people and they kill elephants for meat, or their tusks.

96 Elephant orphanages have been set up in Africa and Asia to look after young elephants. Some of the animals have lost their mothers to poachers. Animal experts rescue them, with the hope that one day they can start new herds and go back to the wild.

▼ These young Asian elephants are in an orphanage. Here they are fed and protected from poachers.

97 Groups of people called conservationists work hard to save elephants. They study elephants to gain a better understanding of how they live. Conservationists hope to find new ways that humans and elephants can live side by side.

▲ This elephant is wearing a radio transmitter. It allows scientists to study how the elephant behaves and where it travels.

98 Scientists study elephants in the wild. They work in reserves, which are special areas that are protected from farmers and poachers. Elephants are fitted with radio transmitters, so scientists can follow their movements over many years.

▲ Tourists flock to African safari parks, where they can watch animals, including elephants, in their natural surroundings.

99 Tourism can bring elephants and people together in a positive way. Thousands of tourists visit countries with elephants every year, bringing money and work for local people. Seeing elephants up close helps people to understand these majestic, beautiful beasts.

100 Teaching people to value elephants is a big step towards protecting them for the future. Schools in Africa and Asia teach children about elephants, and how important they are to the environment. Farmers are taught new ways to protect their crops, without harming hungry elephants.

Index